Guide to Flat ferreting

flat ferreting

Preface

Flat ferreting is what I call the cuteness to owning a ferret it's not like owning any other animal it has its ups and downs. I feel there are different stages to owning ferrets and in this book I hope to show you each step, as well as teach you from preparation to supporting your " Children." If you follow these guidelines you should enjoy your ferret much more. It's almost like having children. I wish you good luck and send you on your way to flat ferreting.

In memory of

Rusty

December 1998

and **Dedicated** to

WarmFuzzy Ferret Rescue

Shirley & Clarence Hertzog-owners

Part of the proceeds of this book will go toward the rescue to help cut the cost of the veterinary bills.

Contents

Preparation

This is the first step to owning a ferret. Remember owning a ferret is a big responsibility. It's not like going out and buying a dog or a cat. Ferrets are like children, they get into mischief and everything to them is like a toy. If you know of anyone who owns a ferret, talk to them and visit them while they have their ferrets out. It's a good practice to write down some questions you feel are important. Questions like, what kind of food do they eat? How do I know when they are sick? How can I train them? And what do I put in there litter box? These are but a few of the questions you should ask.

The next step is to find a ferret rescue close by and make arrangements to visit that rescue. It helps to see first hand just what goes into owning and taking care of these little fuzzies. While you are there you should find out about the veterinarians in the area. As there are some veterinarians that do not know a lot about ferrets. Some rescues do a lot of things they do, like teaching how to clip nails, clean ears, coming up with remedies to make your ferret feel better and much much more. Although they **are not doctors and do not treat or prescribe medicine**, some of them do work with herbs to help the ferrets in many other ways.

Ferret rescues in most cases are able to help you with most of the problems that you face when you own a ferret. They're usually the first source of contact when you have a situation you don't understand. A ferret rescue is usually in the home of the people who take care of them. These people usually have them divided into groups. The first group are the ferrets that belong to them. The second group are the rescue ferrets that are ready for adoption. Then you have the third group and in this group are the ferrets that are being trained to be people friendly.

The rescued ferrets are usually held for a period of time to see what kind of personalities they have. This is very important because in order to adopt ferrets that are people friendly, the rescue has to screen the ferrets. They have to make sure that anything that is wrong with the ferrets are corrected before they go up for adoption. The rescues must see that all the ferrets are up to date on their shots. They also take care of any abuse that the ferret has gone through by nursing them back to health and helping them to become people friendly again. This is the reason that most ferret rescues asked for a donation. It is very costly to rehabilitate a ferret. Some of the rescues have 20 to 40 rescue ferrets plus their own.

The ferret

The ferret is not in the rodent family as many people think. In fact the ferret is in the family with the weasel and the mink. The ferret is **Mustela Puturious Furo** and when you break it down goes as follows;

kingdom - Animalia - life, plants & fungi excluded

Phylum - Chordata - with a spinal cord

Subphylum - Vertebrata - with the background

Class - Mammalia - nurse their young

Subclass - Eutheria - with the placenta, excluding marsupials

Order - carnivore - flesh eaters

Suborder – Fissipeda - with separate toes, excluding seals &   walruses

Family- Mustelidae - those who carry off mice

*****Genus** - mustela - ferrets and their milk

*****Subgenus** - Putorius - European polcats, from the

Latin putor = stench

*****species** - putoius - the domestic ferret

*****species** – Furo - Latin for ferret (fair'-et)

Ferrets are members of the weasel family Musteladae. In Europe, the ferret is the domesticated form of the polecat, Mustela putorus. Since ancient times it has been used to kill rats and drive rabbits from their burrows. The black-footed ferret of the Western United States, Mustela (species meaning black) nigripes, feeds mostly on prairie dogs. Once considered extinct, ferrets bred in captivity have been reintroduced in Wyoming.

Everett Sentman

Bibliography *Seal, U.S. Conservation biology and the black-footed ferret (1989); Wellstead, Graham, ferrets and ferreting (1989)*

Although we refer to the black-footed ferret, it is not the ferret we now breed for domestication in the home. This is like comparing a lion with the house cat. Other differences are that ferrets are not nocturnal animals, they adjust to our daily schedules.

Many years ago in ancient Egypt, ferrets were used to protect the granary. They started out with the pharaohs and the most wealthy who kept them as their pets. The ferrets have been domesticated for over 3000 years and have worked their way through Europe. The domestic ferret is a descendent of the European polecat. Upon coming to the North American continent the farmers use these fuzzy creatures to chase rabbits and other rodents out of their fields barns, silos, vegetable and flower gardens.

The ferret may look like a very delicate animal but don't let it full you. It would stand up to anything many times its size if it had to, especially if it was cornered. It is however just like any other animal if it is injured, cornered or mistreated, it will likely retaliate. This is the exception because the ferret views everything as a toy and it will try to play with it. When treated correctly it can be the most loving of all animals. You can have many hours of fun with these little fuzzies without a recharge.

Don't let it scare you when they go into what we call their little dance. They look like they are trying to throw their back out and back up into anything that gets in their way and they can be most hilarious at these times. It really helps to have at least two ferrets, this way they will have a sleeping buddy, a playmate and they will have a healthier life. If at any time your little fuzzies get out of the cage and room you set aside for them, you can rest assured if you have anything laying around that is small and/or shiny you may not find it until you clean thoroughly. Although these little fuzzies are cute and lovable they hide things like pack rats.

Getting ready

Now you're ready to become an owner of your first bouncing ferret. You'll get hours of fun on one charging no batteries needed.

First you get the room ready that they are going to live in. This is the part we call " ferret proofing" the room. Start by taking out anything that they might get into such as plants, breakables and things they can crawl up on or into. Now we close off the doorway with a piece of plywood or anything that will keep them in the room, about 2 feet is high enough and then you might want to put a piece of 4 or 6 inch PVC pipe on top by cutting a slit in it lengthwise and slipping it over top of the plywood. When a ferret jumps up to try and get out they will slip off of it and soon learn they can't get out. Child gates do not work because ferrets climb these like a latter however, you can use these if you slip Plexiglas in them. The Gates should be at least 2 feet high. And put a piece of PVC over it like you did the plywood.

Now for the cage. The cage is a very important item not to be taken lightly it could mean the difference between having a healthy and happy ferret or a miserable and unhappy and the cage should have enough room for the ferret to sleep and walk around in and it should have a section to keep the litter box and a section away from the litter box where they can eat and drink.

A three level cage approximately 3 to 3 1/2 foot high, 2 1/2 foot long and a foot and a half deep is what I recommend for 2 to 4 ferrets. All levels of the cage should have a linoleum type covering to prevent the ferrets feet from getting sore or cut on the wire shelf of the cage. Full levels are best but a hammock hanging even with a half shelf works well. Remember, the more rug or material you use, the more your cage will smell.

The food dish should be small but heavy ones so they cannot overturn it but, you might want to get a bungee cord to wrap around it to give it extra staying power. You may decide to get a dish that attaches to the cage. The first thing you do is either get Springwater or get a purifier for your faucet. Water bottles should be found at the top or middle level by the food with easy access but, not too close to each other or the ferrets will get their food wet and cause it to mold.

Next thing to think about is the litter box. I find that an oblong litter box about 10 x 14 x 3" is the best. Do not get a triangle box that fits in the corner. The reason is that the male will go once in each of the outside corners than out on the floor. The male's body will usually be too long for the box and will urinate out on the floor of the cage. The box should be cleaned daily.

Do not use scoopable cat letter. The ferret being a very clean animal when washing itself could ingest the litter and clog their digestive tract and then you will see a very large vet Bill. I highly recommend using hardwood stove pellets, they will last a long time and are safer for your ferret and easier to clean.

Now you are ready to get the hammocks installed. The hammock can be a single or a double. My kids like it two ways in the top level they have a single Hammock with a towel draped over it and at the second level they have a type of a hammock that is opens toward the shelf that holds the food dish. Do not use any material that contains a fleece type material in or on it. This material is not good for the ferret because they could ingest the fiber dust. The material you use should be able to breathe. A ferret's body temperature is approximately 101° and therefore should not be under heavy cover. You should not worry about them getting cold but **do** worry about them getting too warm.

Now that you have the cage ready let's work on the room. I suggest that a litter box be placed in each corner and if you have carpet, a piece of linoleum about 10 to 12 inches bigger than the box should be put under it

There are a few ways to deter your kids from going on the floor instead of in the box. One way is to wash their betting and put a small amount of vanilla extract in the water of the rinse cycle. After you put their bedding back in place in their cage, mix a small portion of vanilla extract and water together in a bowl. Take a cloth and dip it in the solution and rub it anywhere you see them going or where you don't want them to start. This will make them think it is their betting and they will not go there.

Another way is to place more bedding or things they play with in the areas you don't want them to go. Remember that they go in corners and under things in dark places.

If you find your ferret going outside the box after you get them home you may have to train them by putting them in the box when you see them going anywhere else. This will help them to know that they must go in the box instead of on the floor or anywhere else. You'll have to do this every time but don't get frustrated, they will eventually learn. Ferrets usually use the litter box when they first wake up, so this is a good time for potty training your ferret.

Foods & treats

Remember this is a ferret and not a dog or cat. You feed it ferret food and not dog or cat food. Dogs and cats require high fiber low fat and low protein diet. Where as ferrets require a low fiber high-fat high-protein diet. I strongly recommend "*Totally Ferret*" as the ferret food to buy. There are probably a couple of other new foods for ferrets out there today. These foods are a little more expensive than the other foods but, in the long run you'll see better performance out of your little fuzzies. Your ferret will not eat as much, their coats will come out better, their teeth will look better and stay cleaner.

When it comes to treats **Tone** is the word, I recommend you buy a bottle of " *Furo - tone*, *Ferret- tone* or *Lina tone*, " they usually come in 8 ounce bottles and mix it with a 16 ounce bottle of virgin olive oil. After mixing the two together in a bowl or some kind of container (both are oil-based so they will mix without any problem), pour some of the mixture back in the tone bottle and the rest in the olive oil bottle and be sure to mark the date on the bottle. It will keep in the refrigerator for a long time (anywhere from 3 to 6 months then discard it). Use the tone bottle to give a treat to the ferret by mouth. Do not put the oil in the food or water because, if you put it in the water it will sour and they won't drink it, if you put it in the food they will not eat it and it will go bad. You can also use the tone to help teach the ferret to do tricks and other things. One word of caution, remember you can " overdose" them so keep the treats to a minimum.

There are a few treats out on the market made for ferrets but most ferrets don't eat them. You will have to do this by trial and error to find out what they will eat. My ferrets like " ***Pounce***" and I can also suggest a treat called" ***Cheweasel***." The cheweasel is a gelatin like substance that is similar to the Sugar Daddy. You can hang it up on a rubber band like string for them to play with and eat. Sometimes I just put them on the floor when the kids are out playing and they use them for a toy and sometimes they will chew on them as they play with them. Another toy and treat that they like to chew on and play with is the chew sticks. They like to chew on these and it also helps them keep their teeth clean and strong.

Now for the Ferret

You can go to a pet shop but in most cases you may not be happy with the results after taking the ferret home. A lot of the stores have inexperienced help and don't know the correct way to take care of the little fuzzies.

A lot of stores I have been in do not have the ferrets in the correct living environment. They do not tell you correctly about the litter box, the correct food, the correct bathing and other hygiene. In essence they give you a little booklet, sell you some or all the products you don't need, give you wrong information and send you on your merry way. In some cases a lucky rescue is going to get your little ferret.

Unfortunately most stores and some farms today are selling them at five weeks because the big breeder farms are pushing them out early to save money and this hurts everyone because the ferrets are not ready to be taken away from the mother or adopted and wind up not to be people friendly.

People who go to the stores to get their ferrets do not know that baby ferrets are not mature enough to be people friendly they bite as to play tag and not to be aggressive.

They need to be handled more and should have other ferrets to play with.

The best way to adopt the ferret is to go to a rescue and have them leave the ferrets run and play. At this time you should try to mix in and play with them and the people at the rescue will help you in picking out the ferrets that are best for you. Don't forget these people have the training you seek to help you find your fuzzy but, remember you don't pick the one you want you let the ferret pick you if at all possible.

If you already have one or more ferrets and are looking for another one take your ferret (s) to the rescue and let them run with the others. The ones that play best with yours are the ones you pick. Remember you are doing this for your fuzzy and not for yourself.

Your new fuzzy

Now that you have your new " bouncing flat ferret" fuzzy home, it's time to start you on your way to disciplining and understanding your ferret.

In holding the ferret, pick it up just in back of the front legs. This is the bending point of your fuzzy. Lay it in your arms like you would a baby put your hand over it with your middle finger on one side and your index finger on the other side of the neck. This is what we call holding time and this teaches the ferret that you are in charge.

At this point there are only two reasons why the ferret wants down. One is to go to the bathroom and the other is to run and get away. Let the ferret down in the litter box but, If he goes to take off pick him up again and put him back in your arm.

This time hold him there until he stops struggling and **you** want to put him down, otherwise the ferret is training you. A sign to watch for is when it gives a " sigh" and wait a few seconds (or the ferret will realize the sigh means to get down). Now let him down to play and about 10 to 15 min. later do the same as before. Do this off and on until he just lays in your arm and doesn't try to get away. This teaches him that you are the boss and the one in charge. This is also when the tone comes in as a treat and if he lays there give him some tone. Don't use the tone to keep him there just use it to acknowledge that he did the right thing, then put him down. Using tone in this manner will help you teach him tricks also.

The more you handle your fuzzy the more people friendly they will become and the less they will nip. If you play with your ferret at least once a day and let it run about an hour a day your ferret will be a happy one. You can do this while you clean their cages.

Disciplining

When disciplining your little fuzzy you must find and stick to a corrective action not meant to hurt but instill the thought" I am not supposed to do this." If you find your little one out of his area or heading into something he shouldn't, just pick him up shake your finger at him saying no. If you find your ferret going to potty where he shouldn't, just pick him up, look him in the eyes and say no, then hiss at him and put him down in the litter box. When the little one nips, pick him up and put him in your arm like a baby then hiss and say no. This would be a good time to do holding time. If the nipping persists, then take the ferret holding it by the shoulder and the head and bite him on the scruff of the neck and turn him to face you and hiss loudly at its face. This is what the mother ferret would do if she were around. When you bite the ferret on the neck you are biting to discipline and not to hurt, so be very careful how hard you bite. Hitting the ferret is on called for and never is it necessary. By using the scruff of the neck either by holding or biting sends enough of a message that something wrong has been done. If you feel you must hit them than hit them lightly on the rear and hold it up and hiss at their face like the mother would do.

Health

An important point to remember is the cleaner you keep your ferret and its environment the longer and healthier life it will live, not to mention the enjoyment you can have with good ferreting. It would be nice to get an air purifier to help keep the air fresher. Some ferrets do have more of a smell than others.

Try to create a schedule of hygiene and stick to it as much as possible. Clean the cage at lease on a daily basis and as for the litter box, scoop the big clumps out and sift the pellets. You may use the waste containing clumps and fine sifted wood particles to put around the flower and vegetable garden to keep the rodents away and this acts as a very good fertilizer also.

Try to use a biodegradable disinfectant to clean the cage because, the least chemically treated environment they live in, the healthier they will be.

Your ferret must have a distemper shot once a year. Distemper is an airborne virus that can enter your house by attaching itself to your clothing and shoes and many other ways. It is recommended to have a rabies shot yearly and you can do that through your veterinarian. When you and your veterinarian get to know each other well enough you may be able to give the distemper shot yourself but, only veterinarians and licensed techs are allowed to give the rabies shot.

When is it time to wash the bedding? When you see the bedding start to turn brown or you still have an odor after cleaning the cage. This would be a good time also to wash your little fuzzy. As for the water and soap bath I recommend that you only do this once or twice a year and do not use a perfumed shampoo or soap because as soon as you're done with its bath your little fuzzy will be rubbing itself on your rugs and furniture trying to get its own smell back. When your ferret gets washed and they don't smell their own essence they will rub themselves on anything until their essence is back and this is one reason why we use the" **dry bath**" most of the time.

There is what we call the dry bath on the market that is much better for your little fuzzy because it does not remove all of the oils off their skin. This dry bath unlike the wet bath leaves just enough oil on their skin to keep it from cracking open and leaving them susceptible to diseases. You can use this bath as often as you like. The dry bath consists of a pouch with a small amount of what I understand to be called cracked bran. This is bran before they put the chemicals to it. You put the ferret in the pouch with his head sticking out and rub your little fuzzy for a minute or two then take your little fuzzy out and brush him good. I would suggest doing this process over a bowl or something to catch the excess bran. I usually tell the people to smell their fuzzy before they give them this bath and again afterwards. After the bath you will see a beautiful shine on your ferret and you might even see him do the ferret dance.

I'll only hit briefly on the nails and ears. The nails should be done approximately every 3 to 4 weeks and approximately three days before the show. You should use small bird nail clippers and clip just in front of the blood vain so you don't make them bleed.

The ear should be cleaned when you give the bath and the night before a show, when they stink or if you see they are paying too much attention to their ears. To clean the ears take warm soapy water in a clean container (a drop or two of a general soap in 2 to 4 ounces of water). Put a couple of drops in the ears and rub it in gently with your fingers. Take a Q-tip and clean the ear out until your Q-tip is clean but be careful when doing this.

The rescue you deal with or your veterinarian will be more than happy to instruct you on the do's and don'ts of nail clipping and ear cleaning. For a small donation your ferret rescue will be more than happy to clip nails, clean teeth and clean their ears for you.

Leashes and harnesses

Let's start with the harness the most important of all. A ferret comes in different sizes, the measurement is taken from the middle of the neck to the area just in back of the shoulder blades and therefore anything with one-size-fits-all does not pertain to your ferret. Most of the harnesses on the market are not made with the ferret in mind. Ferrets come in three basic sizes and they are female, male, and Hob. There are occasions where some males are small enough for a female harness and some females are big enough for a mail harness and that is why we measure from the middle of the neck to the area just in back of the shoulder blades. Before going to a store to get your equipment why not see if your rescue sells what you need or can get it at a lower price for you.

Next we come to the leashes. The lease should be about 36 inches long and it should be made of a light but strong material. A light webbing would be nice and it should have a metal clip on it rather than a plastic clip. If you have two ferrets and don't want to hassle with two leashes and get them all tangled up then get what we call a tandem. A tandem connects to the end of the leash so you can have more control and less entanglement.

In closing

I hope this book gives you an idea of what it takes to own a ferret. I have tried to make it as easy as possible to show you how to start out and what it takes to get you on your way to flat ferreting. Don't forget ferreting is a big responsibility and can be fun as well. See you at the shows.

Good luck

First printing

February 4, 2000

A tribute to

Warmfuzzy ferret rescue

Ferret friendly ferret wise Warmfuzzy has any size

They tickle your inners and tickle your sides

But look out and be advised

These little fuzzies will hypnotize

Warmfuzzie's the best don't get me wrong

I've been to some others and I can't say they're wrong

Come look for yourself and you shall see

In good hands I know you're fuzzies will be

Go over the gate and watch your step

I'm sure when you look you'll find your pet

They're running loose but have no fear

I'm sure your pet will be very near

With batteries charged and the kids running wild

You know you must treat them each like a child

With all of them running one friend you'll make

When it's time to leave that one you'll take

They tell you how to give your fuzzy it's care

Then you go home and you start to prepare

The cages are ready and the ferrets go in

Now go get your rest before the fun can begin

When fuzzies run there at their best

You soon will be put to their little test

Before you put the fuzzies out to play

Did you ferret proof your house today

We hope you enjoy your ferret's dance

No they're not crazy, no not a chance

They're funny and cute without a doubt

There your children now and please don't shout

Warm fuzzy's the name and ferrets the game

Play with our fuzzies and you'll be the same

Good parents we are and you'll be too

If you listen to us and then you do

" Happy Ferreting"

About Rusty

My Rusty was dark eyed white, at least he was supposed to be. When he came into the rescue he had what we think was cigar burns on his back and broken teeth. He was orange in color probably from the wrong type of food. Was he abused?... nah it must have been my imagination.

I had been down in the dumps for couple of days and this one day at that time was the worst day of my life. The place that I worked at had clients that I helped take care of in one way or another. I had been there 6 1/2 years as a full-time volunteer and this was before the information act came to pass. I met a good friend through the office because he was a client of ours and I saw him quite a few times. As time went on he told me about a ferret rescue that he and his wife owned and asked me to come over to see his little fuzzies and this happened a few times.

This one day Clarence came in and walked right by me without asking me to come over and see the ferrets, so I stopped him and asked him why he didn't ask me to come over. He told me that he was tired of asking me all the time and that if I decided to come over I would. Well that day I left early from work and went home and sat on the edge of my bed thinking about all the things that was happening in my life. At that moment I felt so down and blue and I thought I couldn't take it anymore, so I reached under my pillow and pulled out my gun and as I put the gun to my head praying, I had the thought of going over to the rescue to see the ferrets.

I put the gun down and pushed it back under my pillow, got up, put on my coat and hat and went out the door. I went down and got in the car and drove over to the rescue.

When I got there, Shirley let me in and had me go in and sit down on the floor. Shirley and Clarence were talking to a prospective couple who was adopting a ferret. Shirley came back in and took out another ferret, his name was Rusty. When Shirley put Rusty on the floor he came right to me. I picked him up and he just laid in my arms so still. I must have held him for a couple of hours. When I set him down on the floor he wanted to get back up. The funny thing was that he wouldn't go to anyone else when I was there. I had helped nurse him back to health and after of a few weeks he started to look like a dark eyed white again. Because of the time I put in with the rescue and the way I took care of Rusty, Shirley and Clarence made sure I was his daddy.

Eventually Rusty came home with me and by this time Rusty had also made a friend and his name was Fuzzy. We found out that we could not separate them or neither of them would eat (ferret math). Well I guess they both found their way to my heart.

When I moved into my new apartment Rusty and Fuzzy came to live with me. Eventually I had rusty playing like a ferret should. Those kids of mine had worn me out. All I had to start out with was a small cage that Clarence loaned me until I got a cage of my own. I started to go to the shows and help Shirley and Clarence with the rescue. In December of 98 around Christmas we went to the Fort Washington show. Normally I took the kids with me but this time I left them at the rescue. This show's Chinese auction had a big beautiful cage. I didn't take much money along but had enough money to buy a dollar ticket. I said to Shirley and Clarence" I'm going to win that cage for Rusty" and when it came time for the cage to be raffled off I was right there to get my prize. I had written Warmfuzzy on the back of the ticket. I watched as the ticket was pulled and they called warmfuzzy. I was calling out" here I am" and they just ignored me and called for Shirley and Clarence because they only knew them as warmfuzzy. Jim, one of their friends that knew that I was now part of the rescue grabbed the girl that had the mike and told her I was the winner. I was so proud that my kids were going to get their new home.

Shirley said" where are we going to put it" and Clarence said" we'll make room" and we did. On the ride back I was so happy I didn't have a care in the world. When we arrived at the rescue, Shirley went in first to get things ready for the kids to go in the cages. Clarence took some things in and came back out and told me Shirley wanted to talk to me. The first thing I thought of was what did I do this time. As I opened the door I heard what I thought was Shirley crying. I walked to the ferret room and sure enough she was crying her head off. As I turned to look in the room, I asked what was wrong and then I saw the answer. Rusty was lying on a towel on top of the cage all curled up. He must have passed away just before we got home because, he was still warm and soft. Well by this time I heard a duet in perfect harmony. Before we took care of Rusty I left Fuzzy say his goodbyes to his buddy, then we took Rusty out and put him to rest and said a nice prayer for him. He didn't even get to see his cage.

It was about two o'clock in the morning but Shirley and Clarence would not let me leave before I picked another companion for Fuzzy. His new partner was a girl named Potto and I believe she may have been the partner to koto on the movie, "The Beast Master." As of this date Fuzzy has two girlfriends and they are Potto who is three and Samantha five. Now we are a happy family of four (I sold my guns).

The rescues that we get in are not all abused. In some cases they are replaced by other animals or not wanted anymore and a good many of these ferrets are store-bought.

This is the story of only one of the great many rescued ferrets I hope you enjoyed it.

" Rest in peace Rusty "

A special treat

This story came about because of a short story I had written for an advertisement about our ferret shelter that was e-mailed to the FML (ferret mailing list). The main characters are my three ferrets; Potto, Snickers and Snoops and me. I must tell you that they are my pride and joy and I would do anything for them.

In memory of

Rhonda, Rusty, Potto, Fuzzy, Snickers, Snoops and Samantha

Runaway Ferrets

It all started one January morning when I woke to a beautiful winter day. I just crawled out of bed and went into the living room to say good morning to the kids, Potto, Snickers and Snoops. Their cage was right outside my bedroom door and I say good morning to them first thing.

As I went through the doorway and looked at the cage I saw that the cage door was open. I got down on my knees and proceeded to poke around at their sleeping places and to my surprise found the cage to be completely empty. I started to look around in all the rooms and in all their little hiding places but to no avail. My son who was sleeping on my futon in the living room was dead to the world and when I woke him, had no idea of my dilemma. I filled him in on the missing ferrets he got up and off we went to find my little fuzzies.

I just could not understand how they got out of the cage but this was not the time to worry about that. We proceeded to take another look around the apartment with no luck. I told my son to go out in the hall and start at one end and I would go to the other end and we would meet back at my apartment door. We looked every place we could think of that they would hide. In the meantime I met up with a couple of tenant's in the hall and told them of my missing ferrets. They said they would give us a hand to help look for them. Next we went down to the ground floor and made another thorough search.

Even the Secret Service would have been proud of the way we conducted our search. I took a chance and went to the main entrance and looked outside and when I got to the snow at the edge of the pavement I saw three sets of ferret tracks. Well I was relieved to know that they made it this far because I figured it would be easy to track them now that we found their prints. Now it was time to contact the men in blue and see if we could get a tracker to try and follow the tracks I found in the snow. I knew the chief of police and called him to ask him to honor one of my favors he owed me. I told him of my dilemma and asked if he knew someone who was a good tracker. He went to work and in no time he brought in the cavalry and boy you never saw so many flashing lights.

I had my son call the radio station and have them announce my problem with the ferrets. I took my trusty cell phone with me and as we went across the snow toward town I got a call from a listener that he saw what he thought were little furry animals running down the main street of town. They must have had a good head start on us because when we got there they were nowhere to be found. We found more tracks and continued to follow them. Those little tracks lead right up to the shopping mall at the end of town. We continued to follow the very faint tracks of paw prints into the big store at the end of the mall. We asked the store manager if he saw anything strange and his reply was that a couple of customers had mentioned that they saw little animals running loose through the store but he didn't pay any attention and thought it was a joke.

I bumped into a customer that overheard me talking to the manager and he told me that he saw three animals going out of the store carrying a box. He didn't want to say anything because he thought someone might think he was crazy. So off we went outside to try and find more tracks. At that time my son called and told me that another listener called in and said they saw three ferrets carrying a box headed toward my end of town. The chief and I hopped back into the patrol car and headed back to the other end of town to find another set of tracks leading back to the apartment building where I lived. We followed them to the entrance of the building I quickly went upstairs to my apartment and found my son asleep on the futon again.

I looked over at the cage and my jaw dropped to the floor. There were my kids, Potto asleep on the lower hammock, Snickers hanging out of the towel on the upper one and snoops lying upside down under Snickers. I went out in the hall and saw the chief turning the corner and told him that the kids were back and safe as far as I could see. After saying thank you to all I went back in the apartment to give the kids their do. I first went into the bathroom to wash my face from the sweat of the ordeal and as I was coming out I noticed a box on my bed. I walked over and picked it up and under it was a note that read, we love you dad and because you are always getting things for us before yourself and taking good care of us we decided to get you a gift. With love Potto, Snickers and Snoops I put the box down and opened it up and what do you think was in it? Well that will be a secret between the kids and me and how can I punish them after that! I still would like to know how they got out in the first place, I guess that will be their little secret.

The end

If you liked this story and would like to read more of the same, please look for my books called" **Ferret Short Stories**." These stories will put you in the mood for your little fuzzies and are made to bring a smile to your face. You might even see your little one's faces as you read these stories. As I said before happy ferreting and good luck.

This book I dedicate to my children: Niki Elaine, Cynthia Rose, Edward Jr, Anthony LaRay and David John.